1000
INSPIRATIONAL
QUOTES

Daily Inspirational and Motivational Quotations by Famous People About Life, Love, and Success

Table of Contents

Introduction

"Don't resort to imitation but rather look for inspiration to further your own creation in pursuit of innovation."

—Anonymous

Life is never constant; it is a bumpy ride which sometimes takes us to our lowest points. That is the time when most of us lose hope and determination. To regain our inner strength and confidence, we often need to look and learn from past and present examples. Men and women with exemplary characteristics have shown the world how to win true peace, contentment, and real success in life. Where their deeds set an example for all, their words have left indelible marks on people's minds and spirits. Those pearls of inspiration have guided many different individuals to become an inspiration themselves. The text of this book presents yet another set of 1000 of the most inspirational quotes from the most influential personalities of all time, whether it was John C Maxwell, Napoleon Bonaparte, Princess Diana, Lao Tzu, and many others. Each eminent personality quoted in this book excelled in their lives in different ways, but all left a number of lessons worth remembering for those to come.

How To Use This Book

There is no one key to success. Life offers many paths and opportunities, and it is up to us what we grab on to. These inspirational quotes vary in their subject and their source, it is up to us how we incorporate them into our lives, and how we make the best use out of them. Since this book is designed with the sole purpose of inspiring all to the fullest, we share here some quick tips to garner all the benefits from this collection.

1.   Read Thoroughly:

You never know what might inspire you! That is why it is necessary to read the complete content of the book thoroughly. Go through all the quotes in a manner suitable to you. Eventually, you will end up gathering more knowledge than you ever expected.

2.   Use as a Regular Source of Inspiration:

You can set your target to 20-50 quotes a day, or read a single quote a day to learn certain lessons. It gets easier to manage your time doing this, and the reader remains in touch with wise words every day. It all depends on your own mood and energy but try to create a daily habit and constantly motivate yourself through these words.

3. Consistency Is the Key:

Perseverance and consistency always lead to great heights. Whenever reading a quotation book, remember to stay consistent in your efforts and do not give up after reading halfway through. Maybe the part which could have inspired you the most is yet to come. Set a small, yet achievable target.

4. Connect with the Content:

Without relevance, no text can make sense to us. These quotes will look like a mere jumble of words if you aren't able to develop a connection with them. Try to read and think over each one in relation to your life. Only then will you be able to get real inspiration from it.

5. Counter the Challenges:

We can read on and on, but nothing can ever really make a difference unless we push ourselves to the limit. There are plenty of inspirational quotes in this book that call the reader to seek challenges and stand against the odds. They must be willing to face those challenges head on.

John C. Maxwell

To lead any way other than by example, we send a fuzzy picture of leadership to others. If we work on improving ourselves first and make that our primary mission, then others are more likely to follow.

The measure of a leader is not the number of people who serve him but the number of people he serves.

Leaders who are effective are leaders who are disciplined in their daily lives.

A leader is great, not because of his or her power, but because of his or her ability to empower others.

A great leader's courage to fulfill his vision comes from passion, not position.

A leader is one who knows the way, goes the way and shows the way.

Leaders must be close enough to relate to others, but far enough ahead to motivate them.

If you wouldn't follow yourself, why should anyone else?

Anyone can steer the ship, but it takes a leader to chart the course. Leaders who are good navigators are capable of taking their people just about anywhere.

If you want to be a leader, the good news is that you can do it. Everyone has the potential, but it isn't accomplished overnight. It requires perseverance.

Talent is a gift, but the character is a choice.

If you really want to be an uncommon leader, you're going to have to find a way to get much of your vision seen, implemented, and added to by others.

All true leaders have learned to say no to the good in order to say yes to the best.

If you don't change the direction you are going, then you're likely to end up where you're heading.

Sometimes you win, sometimes you learn.

Small disciplines repeated with consistency every day lead to great achievements gained slowly over time.

One of the major keys to success is to keep moving forward on the journey, making the best of the detours and interruptions, turning adversity into advantage.

If we're growing, we're always going to be out of our comfort zone.

The way you live your life today is preparing you for tomorrow. The question is, what are you preparing for?

When people respect you as a person, they admire you. When they respect you as a friend, they love you. When they respect you as a leader, they follow you.

If you want to be the best leader you can possibly be, no matter how much or how little natural leadership talent you possess, you need to become a serving leader.

The challenge of leadership is to create change and facilitate growth.

There are no shortcuts to any place worth going.

The growth and development of people is the highest calling of a leader.

The greatest mistake we make is living in constant fear that we will make one.

What you are going to be tomorrow, you are today.

Success each day should be judged by the seeds sown, not the harvest reaped.

The secret of your success is determined by your daily agenda.

As a leader, the first person I need to lead is me. The first person I should try to change is me.

A difficult time can be more readily endured if we retain the conviction that our existence holds a purpose – a cause to pursue, a person to love, a goal to achieve.

Change is inevitable. Growth is optional.

To lead yourself, use your head; to lead others, use your heart. Always touch a person's heart before you ask him for a hand.

You will never change your life until you change something you do daily. The secret of your success is found in your daily routine.

Courage isn't an absence of fear. It's doing what you are afraid to do. It's having the power to let go of the familiar and forge ahead into new territory.

Growth is the great separator between those who succeed and those who don't.

To change your life, you need to change your priorities.

Successful and unsuccessful people do not vary greatly in their abilities. They vary in their desires to reach their potential.

Leadership is evoking in others the capacity to dream.

Dreams don't work unless you do.

Leaders are meant to help others become the people God created them to be.

John D. Rockefeller

Good leadership consists of showing average people how to do the work of superior people.

If you want to succeed, you should strike out on new paths rather than travel the worn paths of accepted success.

Don't be afraid to give up the good and go for the great.

The way to make money is to buy when blood is running in the streets.

Perseverance can overcome all obstacles. Even the laws of nature cannot stop it.

Charity is injurious unless it helps the recipient to become independent of it.

I always tried to turn every disaster into an opportunity.

He who works all day has no time to make money.

A friendship founded on business is better than a business founded on friendship.

I believe in the dignity of labor, whether with head or hand; that the world owes no man a living, but that it owes every man an opportunity to make a living.

Every right implies a responsibility, every opportunity an obligation, every possession a duty.

I would rather earn 1% off 100 people's efforts than 100% of my own efforts.

If your only goal is to become rich, you will never achieve it.

I believe that it is my duty to make money and use it for the benefit of my neighbors. This is what my conscience tells me.

The road to happiness lies in two simple principles: find what it is that interests you and that you can do well, and when you find it, put your whole soul into it, every bit of energy and ambition and natural ability you have.

Do you know the only thing that brings me pleasure? To see my dividends.

Competition is a sin.

The ability to deal with people is as purchasable a commodity as sugar or coffee, and I will pay more for that ability than for any other under the sun.

How much money does it take to make a man happy? Just one more dollar.

Don't blame the marketing department. The buck stops with the chief executive.

It is wrong to assume that men of immense wealth are always happy.

I have ways of making money that you know nothing of.

The secret of success is to do the common things uncommonly well.

Own nothing, control everything.

God gave me my money.

Think of giving not as a duty but as a privilege.

Giving should be entered into in just the same way as investing.
Giving is investing.

I believe that thrift is essential to well-ordered living.

The most important thing of a young man is to establish credit, a
reputation, and character.

Singleness of purpose is one of the chief essentials for success in life,
no matter what may be one's aim.

John Kennedy

Let every nation know, whether it wishes us well or ill, that we shall pay any price, bear any burden, meet any hardship, support any friend, oppose any foe to assure the survival and the success of liberty.

Conformity is the jailer of freedom and the enemy of growth.

Children are the world's most valuable resource and its best hope for the future.

One person can make a difference, and everyone should try.

Those who dare to fail miserably can achieve greatly.

Ask not what your country can do for you; ask what you can do for your country.

We do these things not because they are easy, but because they are hard.

This country cannot afford to be materially rich and spiritually poor.

I look forward to an America which will not be afraid of grace and beauty.

A nation reveals itself not only by the men it produces but also by the men it honors, the men it remembers.

Our problems are man-made. Therefore, they may be solved by man. No problem of human destiny is beyond human beings.

The goal of education is the advancement of knowledge and the dissemination of truth.

It is time for a new generation of leadership to cope with new problems and new opportunities, for there is a new world to be won.

The human mind is our fundamental resource.

Change is the law of life, and those who look only to the past or the present are certain to miss the future.

The problems of the world cannot possibly be solved by skeptics or cynics whose horizons are limited by the obvious realities. We need men who can dream of things that never were and ask, "Why not?"

Things do not happen. Things are made to happen.

Efforts and courage are not enough without purpose and direction.

If a free society cannot help the many who are poor, it cannot save the few who are rich.

A man may die, nations may rise and fall, but an idea lives on.

Once you say you're going to settle for second, that's what happens to you in life.

The courage of life is often a less dramatic spectacle than the courage of a final moment, but it is no less a magnificent mixture of triumph and tragedy.

Every accomplishment starts with the decision to try.

Let us never negotiate out of fear, but let us never fear to negotiate.

Our progress as a nation can be no swifter than our progress in education. The human mind is our fundamental resource.

Man is still the most extraordinary computer of all.

Julia Child

Just speak very loudly and quickly, and state your position with utter conviction, as the French do, and you'll have a marvelous time!

When you flip anything, you just have to have the courage of your convictions, particularly if it's sort of a loose mass like this.

Find something you're passionate about and keep tremendously interested in it.

This is my invariable advice to people: learn how to cook, try new recipes, learn from your mistakes, be fearless, and above all have fun!

The only real stumbling block is fear of failure. In cooking, you've got to have a what-the-hell attitude.

You'll never know everything about anything, especially something you love.

The measure of achievement is not winning awards. It's doing something that you appreciate, something you believe is worthwhile. I think of my strawberry soufflé. I did that at least 28 times before I finally conquered it.

A cookbook is only as good as its poorest recipe.

If you're in a good profession, it's hard to get bored, because you're never finished—there will always be work you haven't yet done.

If everything doesn't happen quite the way you'd like, it doesn't make too much difference, because you can fix it.

Maybe the cat has fallen into the stew, or the lettuce has frozen, or the cake has collapsed—eh bien, twant pies! [well, too bad!] Usually, one's cooking is better than one thinks it is. And if the food is truly vile, as my ersatz eggs Florentine surely were, then the cook must simply grit her teeth and bear it with a smile and learn from her mistakes.

Always start out with a larger pot than what you think you need.

Katherine Mansfield

The truth is that every true admirer of the novels cherishes the happy thought that he alone, reading between the lines, has become the secret friend of their author.

Could we change our attitude, we should not only see life differently, but life itself would come to be different.

Make it a rule of life never to regret and never to look back. Regret is an appalling waste of energy; you can't build on it. It's only good for wallowing in.

There are always these moments in life when the limits of suffering are reached, and we become heroes and heroines.

The pleasure of all reading is doubled when one lives with another who shares the same books.

In fact, isn't it a joy (there is hardly a greater one) to find a new book, a living book, and to know that it will remain with you while life lasts?

I adore life. What do all the fool's matter and all the stupidity? They do matter, but somehow, for me, they cannot touch the body of life. Life is marvelous. I want to be deeply rooted in it — to live, to expand, to breathe in it, to rejoice, to share it. To give and to be asked for love.

If only one could tell true love from false love as one can tell mushrooms from toadstools.

The mind I love must have wild places, a tangled orchard where dark damsons drop in the heavy grass, an overgrown little wood, the chance of a snake or two, a pool that nobody's fathomed the depth of, and paths threaded with flowers planted by the mind.

I always felt that the great high privilege, relief, and comfort of friendship was that one had to explain nothing.

I want to be all that I am capable of becoming.

The mind I love must have wild places.

How idiotic civilization is! Why be given a body if you have to keep it shut up in a case like a rare, rare fiddle?

Everything in life that we really accept undergoes a change.

Do the hardest thing on earth for you — act for yourself.

Whenever I prepare for a journey, I prepare as though for death. Should I never return, all is in order.

It is of immense importance to learn to laugh at ourselves.

How hard it is to escape from places. However carefully one goes, they hold you, you leave little bits of yourself fluttering on the fences like rags and shreds of your very life.

Make it a rule of life never to regret and never to look back.

To acknowledge the presence of fear is to give birth to failure.

You have never been curious about me; you never wanted to explore my soul.

Ah, what happiness it is to be with people who are all happy, to press hands, press cheeks, smile into eyes.

Looking back, I imagine I was always writing. Twaddle, it was too. But better far write twaddle or anything, anything, than nothing at all.

Lao Tzu

If you correct your mind, the rest of your life will fall into place.

The best fighter is never angry.

A man with outward courage dares to die: a man with inner courage dares to live.

A journey of a thousand miles begins with a single step.

Knowing others is wisdom; knowing yourself is enlightenment.

Care about what other people think, and you will always be their prisoner.

If you are depressed, you are living in the past; if you are anxious, you are living in the future; if you are at peace, you are living in the present.

Mastering others is a strength; mastering yourself is true power.

Be content with what you have, rejoice in the way things are. When you realize there is nothing lacking, the whole world belongs to you.

If you do not change direction, you may end up where you are heading.

A leader is best when people barely know he exists. When his work is done, his aim fulfilled, they will say: we did it ourselves.

Stop thinking and end your problems.

New beginnings are disguised as painful endings.

Manifest plainness, embrace simplicity, reduce selfishness, have few desires.

Make your heart like a lake with a calm, still surface, and great depths of kindness.

Great acts are made up of small deeds.

Life is a series of natural and spontaneous changes. Don't resist them; that only creates sorrow. Let reality be a reality. Let things flow naturally forward in whatever way they like.

He who is contented is rich.

When I let go of what I am, I become what I might be.

To a mind that is still, the whole universe surrenders.

The heart that gives, gathers.

Confidence is the greatest friend.

When you are content to be simply yourself and don't compare or compete, everybody will respect you.

Silence is a source of great strength.

Be still like a mountain, and flow like a great river.

Act without expectation.

Use the light that is within you to revert to your natural clearness of sight.

Give a man a fish, and you feed him for a day. Teach a man to fish, and you feed him for a lifetime.

Watch your thoughts; they become your words. Watch your words; they become your actions. Watch your actions; they become your habits. Watch your habits; they become your character. Watch your character; it becomes your destiny.

Knowledge is a treasure, but practice is the key to it.

Health is the greatest possession.

Empty yourself of everything—let the mind become still.

By letting go, it all gets done.

Margaret Sanger

A free race cannot be born to slave mothers. A woman cannot choose but give a measure of that bondage to her sons and daughters.

The most merciful thing that the large family does to one of its infant members is to kill it.

The most urgent problem today is how to limit and discourage the over-fertility of the mentally and physically defective.

How are we to breed a race of human thoroughbreds unless we follow the same plan? We must make this country into a garden of children instead of a disorderly back lot overrun with human weeds.

No more children should be born when the parents, though healthy themselves, find that their children are physically or mentally defective.

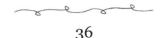

No woman shall have the legal right to bear a child, and no man shall have the right to become a father, without a permit for parenthood.

No permit for parenthood shall be valid for more than one birth.

Margaret Thatcher

Disciplining yourself to do what you know is right and important, although difficult, is the highroad to pride, self-esteem, and personal satisfaction.

If you lead a country like Britain, a strong country, a country which has taken the lead in world affairs in good times and in bad, a country that is always reliable, then you have to have a touch of iron about you.

If you want something said, ask a man; if you want something done, ask a woman.

If you set out to be liked, you would be prepared to compromise on anything at any time, and you would achieve nothing.

To cure the British disease with socialism was like trying to cure leukemia with leeches.

I've got a woman's ability to stick to a job and get on with it when everyone else walks off and leaves it.

You and I come by road or rail, but economists travel on infrastructure.

Any leader has to have a certain amount of steel in them, so I am not that put out being called the Iron Lady.

You may have to fight a battle more than once to win it.

To wear your heart on your sleeve isn't a very good plan; you should wear it inside, where it functions best.

The facts of life are conservative.

It is not the creation of wealth that is wrong, but the love of money for its own sake.

Freedom will destroy itself if it is not exercised within some sort of moral framework, somebody of shared beliefs, some spiritual heritage transmitted through the Church, the family, and the school.

Of course, to be a mother and a housewife is a vocation of a very high kind, but I simply felt that it was not the whole of my vocation. I knew that I also wanted a career. A phrase that Irene Ward, MP for Lynemouth, and I often used to be that, "While the home must always be the center of one's life, it should not be the boundary of one's ambitions."

Plan your work for today and every day, then work your plan.

It may be the cock that crows, but it is the hen that lays the eggs.

Every family should have the right to spend their money, after-tax, as they wish, and not as the government dictates. Let us extend choice, extend the will to choose, and the chance to choose.

It's passionately interesting for me that the things that I learned in a small town, in a very modest home, are just the things that I believe have won the election.

When people are free to choose, they choose freedom.

You don't tell deliberate lies, but sometimes you have to be evasive.

Look at a day when you are supremely satisfied at the end. It's not a day when you lounge around doing nothing; it's a day you've had everything to do, and you've done it.

Power is like being a lady—if you have to tell people you are, you aren't.

It pays to know the enemy, not least because, at some time, you may have the opportunity to turn him into a friend.

Do you know that one of the great problems of our age is that we are governed by people who care more about feelings than they do about thoughts and ideas?

Christmas is a day of meaning and traditions, a special day spent in the warm circle of family and friends.

Europe was created by history. America was created by philosophy.

There are significant differences between the American and European versions of capitalism. The American traditionally emphasizes the need for limited government, light regulations, low taxes, and maximum labor-market flexibility. Its success has been shown, above all, in the ability to create new jobs, in which it is consistently more successful than Europe.

What Britain needs is an iron lady.

Marilyn Monroe

Always remember to smile and look up at what you got in life.

A wise girl knows her limits; a smart girl knows that she has none.

Just because you fail once doesn't mean you're going to fail at everything.

That's the way you feel when you're beaten inside; you don't feel angry at those who've beaten you, you just feel ashamed.

I don't stop when I'm tired. I only stop when I'm done.

A strong man doesn't have to be dominant toward a woman. He doesn't match his strength against a woman weak with love for him. He matches it against the world.

You believe lies, so you eventually learn to trust no one but yourself.

I live to succeed, not to please you or anyone else.

The nicest thing for me is sleep, then at least I can dream.

I don't mind making jokes, but I don't want to look like one.

I have feelings too. I am still human. All I want is to be loved, for myself and for my talent.

It is better to be hated for what you are than to be loved for what you are not.

A friend tells you what you want to hear; a best friend tells you the truth.

This life is what you make it. No matter what, you're going to mess up sometimes, it's a universal truth. But the good part is you get to decide how you're going to mess it up. Girls will be your friends; they'll act like it anyway. But just remember, some come, some go. The ones that stay with you through everything, they're your true best friends. Don't let go of them.

Always, always, always believe in yourself. Because if you don't, then who will, sweetie?

It's far better to be unhappy alone than unhappy with someone—so far.

Keep smiling because life is a beautiful thing, and there's so much to smile about.

We are all stars, but we must learn how to shine.

I believe that everything happens for a reason. People change so that you can learn to let go, things go wrong so that you appreciate them when they're right, you believe lies so you eventually learn to trust no one but yourself, and sometimes good things fall apart so better things can fall together.

I think that love and work are the only things that really happen to us.

Imperfection is beauty, madness is genius, and it's better to be absolutely ridiculous than absolutely boring.

I'm pretty but not beautiful. I sin, but I'm not the devil. I'm good, but I'm not an angel.

Always be yourself. Retain individuality; listen to the truest part of yourself.

To all the girls that think you're fat: because you're not a size zero, you're the beautiful one. It's society who's ugly.

I am not a victim of emotional conflicts. I am human.

It's nice to be included in people's fantasies, but you also like to be accepted for your own sake.

Sweetie, if you're going to be two-faced, at least make one of them pretty.

Be real, be yourself, be unique, be true, be honest, be humble, be happy.

I want to grow old without facelifts. I want to have the courage to be loyal to the face I have made.

If you can't handle me at my worst, you don't deserve me at my best.

Everyone's a star and deserves the right to twinkle.

I want to do the best that I can do at that moment, when the camera starts until it stops.

I think there are two things in human beings: that they want to be alone, but they also want to be together.

Marlene Dietrich

It's the friends you can call up at 4 a.m. that matter.

I love quotations because it is a joy to find thoughts one might have, beautifully expressed with much authority by someone recognized wiser than oneself.

I do not think we have a right to happiness. If happiness happens, say thanks.

Most women set out to try to change a man, and when they have changed him, they do not like him.

Think twice before burdening a friend with a secret.

Love for the joy of loving, and not for the offerings of someone else's heart.

Courage and grace are formidable mixtures. The only place to see it is the bullring.

What remains is solitude.

It is a joy to find thoughts one might have beautifully expressed by someone wiser than oneself.

You're never lonely with a book.

Without tenderness, a man is uninteresting.

The weak are more likely to make the strong weak than the strong are likely to make the weak strong.

A king, realizing his incompetence, can either delegate or abdicate his duties. A father can do neither.

If only sons could see the paradox, they would understand the dilemma.

Mike Tyson

Everybody thinks this is a tough man's sport. This is not a tough man's sport. This is a thinking man's sport. A tough man is going to get hurt really bad in this sport.

Everyone says I wish I was in your shoes. The hundreds of people that wish they were in my shoes don't know the tenth of it. If they were in my shoes, they would cry like a baby.

When you have something in life that you want to accomplish, great. You have to be willing to give up your happiness. I've lost all my sensitivity as far as being embarrassed, being shy, you just have to lose that.

Discipline, doing what you hate to do, but do it as you love it.

I'll fight anybody my trainer puts me in with because I'm confident I can beat any fighter in the world. If anybody can see, I'm almost a master at evading punches coming at me.

I just have this thing inside me that wants to eat and conquer. Maybe it's egotistical, but I have it in me. I don't want to be a tycoon. I just want to conquer people and their souls.

It doesn't faze me what anyone says about me. It doesn't matter what anyone says about me. I'm a totally different entity to what other people think. Michael and Tyson are two different people. I'm Tyson here.

We live in a society where we basically live and strive for what people think about us. We're more visual people, so what we see is basically what we believe, which is not necessarily true.

Unfortunately, sometimes, you can't have fun accomplishing your goals. Sometimes people don't have the determination, the will, the steadfastness, the tenacity; they give in under the slightest struggle.

It's good to be successful and have financial status, but if you're only going to live for the money, you're only going to reach a certain status, and I'm in there for greatness and peace of mind.

I'm a dreamer. I have to dream and reach for the stars, and if I miss a star, then I grab a handful of clouds.

Another thing that freaks me out is time. Time is like a book. You have a beginning, a middle, and an end. It's just a cycle.

Everyone has a plan 'till they get punched in the mouth.

Muhammad Ali

Service to others is the rent you pay for your room here on earth.

He who is not courageous enough to take risks will accomplish
nothing in life.

You could be the world's best garbage man, the world's best model; it
doesn't matter what you do if you're the best.

Jokes? There are no jokes. The truth is the funniest joke of all.

Wouldn't it be a beautiful world if just 10 percent of the people who
believe in the power of love would compete with one another to see
who could do the most good for the most people?

What I suffered physically was worth what I've accomplished in life.

Every day is different, and some days are better than others, but no matter how challenging the day, I get up and live it.

I had it in my heart. I believed in myself, and I had confidence. I knew how to do it, had natural talent, and I pursued it.

Don't count the days, make the days count.

Success is not achieved by winning all the time. Real success comes when we rise after we fall.

I hated every minute of training, but I said, don't quit. Suffer now and live the rest of your life as a champion.

It isn't the mountains ahead to climb that wear you out; it's the pebble in your shoe.

Only a man who knows what it is like to be defeated can reach down to the bottom of his soul and come up with the extra ounce of power it takes to win when the match is even.

You don't lose if you get knocked down; you lose if you stay down.

I can't see what God's plan is. I just know I've got to live with it.

There are billions of people in the world, and every one of them is special. No one else in the world is like you.

Whoever knocks persistently ends by entering.

I do a lot of reading, a lot of studying. I ask questions, I'll go out, travel to these countries, I'll watch how their people live, and I learn.

I run on the road long before I dance under the lights.

Christians are my brothers, Hindus are my brothers, all of them are my brothers. We just think different and believe different.

No one starts out on top. You have to work your way up.

I try not to speak about all the charities and people I help because I believe we can only be truly generous when we expect nothing in return.

There's nothing wrong with getting knocked down, as long as you get right back up.

Enjoy your children, even when they don't act the way you want them to.

A man who views the world the same at 50 as he did at 20 has wasted 30 years of his life.

A man who has no imagination has no wings.

To be a great champion, you must believe you are the best. If not, pretend you are.

It's a lack of faith that makes people afraid of meeting challenges, and I believed in myself.

People will know you're serious when you produce.

Children make you want to start life over.

Old age is just a record of one's whole life.

You're not going to enjoy every minute of the journey, but the success you'll find at the end will make it all worth it.

Champions come and go, but to be legendary, you got to have heart, more heart than the next man, more than anyone in the world.

I am an ordinary man who worked hard to develop the talent I was given.

Wars of nations are fought to change maps. But wars of poverty are fought to map change.

The one without dreams is the one without wings.

What counts in the ring is what you can do after you're exhausted. The same is true in life.

Whatever the challenge was, however unattainable the goal may have seemed, I never let anyone talk me out of believing in myself.

We all have to take defeats in life.

True success is reaching our potential without compromising our values.

To be able to give away riches is mandatory if you wish to possess them. This is the only way that you will be truly rich.

It's hard to beat a guy when he's got his mind made up that he's going to win.

Once the choice is made, do not look back, do not second-guess your decisions.

Live every day as if it were your last because someday, you're going to be right.

What you are thinking about is what you are becoming.

Rest but never quit. Even the sun has a sinking spell each evening. But it always rises the next morning.

Even the greatest was once a beginner. Don't be afraid to take that first step.

I try to learn as much as I can because I know nothing compared to what I need to know.

Nancy Astor

We, women, talk too much, but even then, we don't tell half what we know.

Women have got to make the world safe for men since men have made it so darned unsafe for women.

Real education should educate us out of self into something far finer; into a selflessness which links us with all humanity.

My vigor, vitality, and cheek repel me. I am the kind of woman I would run from.

One reason why I don't drink is that I wish to know when I am having a good time.

The penalty for success is to be bored by the people who used to snub you.

The main dangers in this life are the people who want to change everything—or nothing.

Pioneers may be picturesque figures, but they are often rather lonely ones.

Napoleon Bonaparte

Once you have made up your mind, stick to it; there is no longer any 'if' or 'but.'

You become strong by defying defeat and by turning loss and failure into success.

Let France have good mothers, and she will have good sons.

Death is nothing, but to live defeated and inglorious is to die daily.

The fool has one great advantage over a man of sense; he is always satisfied with himself.

Never interrupt your enemy when he is making a mistake.

Great ambition is the passion of a great character. Those endowed with it may perform very good or very bad acts. It all depends on the principles which direct them.

Friends must always be treated as if, one day, they might be enemies.

Nothing is more difficult, and therefore more precious than to be able to decide.

Until you spread your wings, you'll have no idea how far you can fly.

Impossible is a word found only in the dictionary of fools.

Riches do not consist in possession of treasures, but in use made of them.

You must not fight too often with one enemy, or you will teach him all your art of war.

History is a set of lies agreed upon.

The stupid speak of the past, the wise of the present, and fools of the future.

A society without religion is like a vessel without a compass.

One must change one's tactics every ten years if one wishes to maintain one's superiority.

There are only two forces that unite men—fear and interest.

Death is nothing, but to live defeated and inglorious is to die daily.

A leader is a dealer in hope.

We walk faster when we walk alone.

A true man hates no one.

The surest way to remain poor is to be an honest man.

Take time to deliberate, but when the time for action has arrived,
stop thinking and go.

If you want a thing done well, do it yourself.

He who fears being conquered is sure of defeat.

Imagination rules the world.

Napoleon Hill

Success comes to those who become success conscious.

There are no limitations to the mind except those we acknowledge, both poverty and riches are the offspring of thought.

Most great people have achieved their greatest success, just one step beyond their greatest failure.

Any idea, plan, or purpose may be placed in the mind through repetition of thought.

Our minds become magnetized with the dominating thoughts we hold in our minds, and these magnets attract to us the forces, the people, the circumstances of life which harmonize with the nature of our dominating thoughts.

When your desires are strong enough, you will appear to possess superhuman powers to achieve.

The starting point of all achievement is desire. Keep this constantly in mind. Weak desires bring weak results, just as a small fire makes a small amount of heat.

A goal is a dream with a deadline.

Opportunity often comes disguised in the form of misfortune or temporary defeat.

Whatever your mind can conceive and believe, it can achieve.

Every adversity, every failure, every heartbreak, carries with it the seed of an equal or greater benefit.

Great achievement is usually born of great sacrifice, and never the result of selfishness.

Everyone faces defeat. It may be a stepping-stone or a stumbling block, depending on the mental attitude with which it is faced.

If you do not conquer self, you will be conquered by self.

It is literally true that you can succeed best and quickest by helping others succeed.

Success is good at any age, but the sooner you find it, the longer you will enjoy it.

It takes half your life before you discover life is a do-it-yourself project.

Set your mind on a definite goal and observe how quickly the world stands aside to let you pass.

You have a brain and mind of your own. Use it and reach your own decisions.

Victory is always possible for the person who refuses to stop fighting.

If you do not see great riches in your imagination, you will never see them in your bank balance.

When defeat comes, accept it as a signal that your plans are not sound, rebuild those plans, and set sail once more toward your coveted goal.

A positive mind finds a way it can be done; a negative mind looks for all the ways it can't be done.

Do it now!

The way of success is the way of continuous pursuit of knowledge.

Don't wait. The time will never be just right. Start where you stand and work with whatever tools you may have at your command, and better tools will be found as you go along.

Deliberately seek the company of people who influence you to think and act on building the life you desire.

You are the master of your destiny. You can influence, direct, and control your own environment. You can make your life what you want it to be.

Strength and growth come only through continuous effort and struggle.

Most so-called failures are only temporary defeats.

Fears are nothing more than a state of mind.

The ladder of success is never crowded at the top.

Our only limitations are those we set up in our minds.

The cause of depression is traceable directly to the worldwide habit of trying to reap without sowing.

The more you give, the more comes back to you.

The man who does more than he is paid for will soon be paid for more than he does.

Think twice before you speak, because your words and influence will plant the seed of either success or failure in the mind of another.

Create a definite plan for carrying out your desire and begin at once, whether you are ready or not, to put this plan into action.

Some people dream of success, while others wake up and work hard at it.

You might remember well that nothing can bring you success but yourself.

The majority of men meet with failure of their lack of persistence in creating new plans to take the place of those which fail.

All achievements, all earned riches, have their beginning in an idea.

When you have talked yourself into what you want, right there is the place to stop talking and begin saying it with deeds.

If you give up before your goal is reached, you're a quitter. A quitter never wins, and a winner never quits.

Patience, persistence, and perspiration make an unbeatable combination for success.

There is one quality which one must possess to win, and that is definiteness of purpose, the knowledge of what one wants, and a burning desire to possess it.

Plan your work and work your plan.

Tell me how you use your spare time and how you spend your money, and I will tell you where and what you will be in ten years from now.

Oprah Winfrey

Don't worry about being successful but work toward being

significant, and the success will naturally follow.

Surround yourself only with people who are going to take you higher.

Turn your wounds into wisdom.

Where there is no struggle, there is no strength.

Do the one thing you think you cannot do. Fail at it. Try again. Do

better the second time. The only people who never tumble are those

who never mount the high wire. This is your moment. Own it.

We can't become what we need to be by remaining what we are.

As you become more clear about who you really are, you'll be better able to decide what is best for you—the first time around.

The more you praise and celebrate your life, the more there is in life to celebrate.

Listen to the rhythm of your own calling and follow that.

Be thankful for what you have; you'll end up having more. If you concentrate on what you don't have, you will never have enough.

The greatest discovery of all time is that a person can change their future by merely changing their attitude.

You become what you believe.

I don't think of myself as a poor, deprived ghetto girl who made good. I think of myself as somebody who, from an early age, knew I was responsible for myself, and I had to make good.

Use your life to serve the world, and you will find that it also serves you.

Failure is a great teacher. If you're open to it, every mistake has a lesson to offer.

What I know is that if you do work that you love, and the work fulfills you, the rest will come.

You can have it all. Just not at once.

Luck is a matter of preparation meeting opportunity.

Go ahead, fall down. The world looks different from the ground.

All my life, I have wanted to lead people to an empathy space—to a gratitude space. I want us all to fulfill our greatest potential. To find our calling and summon the courage to live it.

You know you are on the road to success if you would do your job and not be paid for it.

Failing is another stepping stone to greatness.

Follow your instincts. That is where true wisdom manifests itself.

You cannot hate other people without hating yourself.

The biggest adventure you can ever take is to live the life of your dreams.

The big secret in life is there is no secret. Whatever your goal, you can get there if you're willing to work.

Whatever you fear the most has no power; it is your fear that has no power.

Create the highest, grandest vision for your life. Then let every step move you in that direction.

The way through the challenge is to get still, and ask yourself, "What is the next right move?"

The truth is I have, from the very beginning, listened to my instincts. All of my best decisions in life have come because I was attuned to what really felt like the next right move for me.

I don't believe in failure. Failure is just information and an opportunity to change your course.

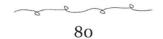

You get in life what you have the courage to ask for.

There is a flow with your name on it. Your job is to find it and let it carry you to the next level.

Doing the best at this moment puts you in the best place for the next moment.

The smallest change in perspective can transform a life. What tiny attitude adjustment might turn your world around?

The single greatest thing you can do to change your life today would be to start being grateful for what you have right now.

Trust that everything happens for a reason, even when you're not wise enough to see it.

Don't settle for a relationship that won't let you be yourself.

No experience is ever wasted. Everything has meaning.

The choice to be excellent begins with aligning your thoughts and words with the intention to require more from yourself.

Often, we don't even realize who we're meant to be because we're so busy trying to live out someone else's ideas. But other people and their opinions hold no power in defining our destiny.

Passion is energy. Feel the power that comes from focusing on what excites you.

With every experience, you alone are painting your own canvas, thought by thought, choice by choice.

I believe that one of life's greatest risks is never daring to risk.

What material success does is provide you with the ability to concentrate on other things that really matter; and that is being able to make a difference, not only in your own life, but in other people's lives.

Oscar Wilde

Keep love in your heart. A life without it is like a sunless garden when the flowers are dead.

The world is divided into two classes, those who believe the incredible, and those who do the improbable.

I have the simplest tastes. I am always satisfied with the best.

A man who does not think for himself does not think at all.

When I was young, I thought that money was the most important thing in life; now that I am old, I know that it is.

The truth is rarely pure and never simple.

Always forgive your enemies—nothing annoys them so much.

There are only two tragedies in life: one is not getting what one wants, and the other is getting it.

There is no sin except stupidity.

I have nothing to declare except my genius.

The only difference between the saint and the sinner is that every saint has a past, and every sinner has a future.

There are only two kinds of people who are really fascinating—people who know absolutely everything, and people who know absolutely nothing.

Success is a science; if you have the conditions, you get the result.

Whenever a man does a thoroughly stupid thing, it is always from the noblest motives.

Life is far too important a thing ever to talk seriously about.

Deceiving others. That is what the world calls a romance.

He has no enemies but is intensely disliked by his friends.

There is only one thing in life worse than being talked about, and that is not being talked about.

If there was less sympathy in the world, there would be less trouble in the world.

What is a cynic? A man who knows the price of everything and the value of nothing.

I am not young enough to know everything.

Men always want to be a woman's first love—women like to be a man's last romance.

Consistency is the last refuge of the unimaginative.

I never travel without my diary. One should always have something sensational to read on the train.

A work of art is the unique result of a unique temperament.

Life is never fair, and perhaps it is a good thing for most of us that it is not.

Whenever people agree with me, I always feel I must be wrong.

Everybody who is incapable of learning has taken to teaching.

It is what you read when you don't have to that determines what you will be when you can't help it.

The world has grown suspicious of anything that looks like a happily married life.

There is always something ridiculous about the emotions of people whom one has ceased to love.

Experience is simply the name we give our mistakes.

As long as a woman can look ten years younger than her own daughter, she is perfectly satisfied.

Between men and women, there is no friendship possible. There is passion, enmity, worship, love, but no friendship.

Women are made to be loved, not understood.

Those who find ugly meanings in beautiful things are corrupt without being charming. This is a fault.

Questions are never indiscreet, answers sometimes are.

Paracelsus

The art of healing comes from nature, not from the physician. Therefore, the physician must start from nature, with an open mind.

Dreams must be heeded and accepted. For a great many of them come true.

Man is a microcosm, or a little world, because he is an extract from all the stars and planets of the whole firmament, from the earth and the elements, and so he is their quintessence.

There is an earthly sun, which is the cause of all heat, and all who are able to see may see the sun; and those who are blind and cannot see him may feel his heat. There is an Eternal Sun, which is the source of all wisdom, and those whose spiritual senses have awakened to life will see that sun and be conscious of His existence; but those who have not attained spiritual consciousness may yet feel His power by an inner faculty which is called Intuition.

The human body is vapor materialized by sunshine mixed with the life of the stars.

Poison is in everything, and nothing is without poison. The dosage makes it either a poison or a remedy.

Fasting is the greatest remedy—the physician within.

Truly it has been said that there is nothing new under the sun, for knowledge is revealed and is submerged again, even as a nation rises and falls. Here is a system, tested throughout the ages, but lost again and again by ignorance or prejudice, in the same way that great nations have risen and fallen and been lost to history beneath the desert sands and in the ocean depths.

Nothing is hidden so much that it wouldn't be revealed through its fruit.

The art of medicine cannot be inherited, nor can it be copied from books

It should be forbidden and severely punished to remove cancer by cutting, burning, cautery, and other fiendish tortures. It is from nature that the disease comes, and from nature comes the cure, not from physicians.

Medicine is not only a science; it is also an art. It does not consist of compounding pills and plasters; it deals with the very processes of life, which must be understood before they may be guided.

The right dose differentiates a poison from a remedy

Man is ill because he is never still.

In every human being, there is special heaven, whole and unbroken.

Know that the philosopher has power over the stars and not the stars over him.

Once a disease has entered the body, all parts which are healthy must fight it: not one alone, but all. Because a disease might mean their common death. Nature knows this, and Nature attacks the disease with whatever help she can muster.

The main reason for healing is love.

Magic has the power to experience and fathom things that are inaccessible to human reason. For magic is great secret wisdom, just as reason is a great public folly.

Medicine rests upon four pillars—philosophy, astronomy, alchemy, and ethics.

Anyone who imagines that all fruits ripen at the same time as the strawberries know nothing about grapes.

From time immemorial artistic insights have been revealed to artists in their sleep and in dreams so that, at all times, they ardently desired them.

That which lives on reason lives against the spirit.

All things are poisons, for there is nothing without poisonous qualities. It is only the dose that makes a thing poison.

Whether wine is a nourishment, medicine, or poison is a matter of dosage.

A little bit of beer is divine medicine.

All that man needs for health and healing has been provided by God in nature; the challenge of science is to find it.

Time is a brisk wind, for each hour it brings something new; but who can understand and measure its sharp breath, its mystery, and its design?

Every physician must be rich in knowledge, and not only of that which is written in books; his patients should be his book, they will never mislead him.

Princess Diana

The greatest problem in the world today is intolerance. Everyone is so intolerant of each other.

I'd like to be a queen in people's hearts.

Only do what your heart tells you.

Nothing brings me more happiness than trying to help the most vulnerable people in society. It is a goal and an essential part of my life—a kind of destiny. Whoever is in distress can call on me. I will come running wherever they are.

Carry out a random act of kindness, with no expectation of reward, safe in the knowledge that, one day, someone might do the same for you.

When you are happy, you can forgive a great deal.

I want to walk into a room, be it a hospital for the dying or a hospital for sick children. I want to do, not just to be.

The biggest disease this day and age is that of people feeling unloved.

Hugs can do great amounts of good, especially for children.

I don't go by the rulebook; I lead from the heart, not the head.

So many people supported me through my public life, and I will never forget them.

Anywhere I see suffering, that is where I want to be, doing what I can.

Everyone needs to be valued.

Family is the most important thing in the world.

Everyone has the potential to give something back.

I touch people. I think everyone needs that.

Helping people in need is a good and essential part of my life.

I think every strong woman in history has had to walk down a similar path, and I think it's the strength that causes confusion and fear.

I like to be a free spirit. Some don't like that, but that's the way I am.

Two things stand like stone: kindness in another's trouble, courage in your own.

If you find someone you love in life, you must hang onto it and look after it; you must protect it.

A mother's arms are more comforting than anyone else's.

Every one of us needs to show how much we care for each other, and in the process, care for ourselves.

I knew what my job was; it was to go out and meet the people and love them.

Pythagoras

Be silent or let thy words be worth more than silence.

The oldest, shortest words—yes and no—are those who require the most thought.

Rest satisfied with doing well, and leave others to talk of you as they please.

Friends are as companions on a journey who ought to aid each other to persevere on the road to a happier life.

Wisdom thoroughly learned will never be forgotten.

Do not say a little in many words but a great deal in a few.

There is geometry in the humming of the strings; there is music in the spacing of the spheres.

A fool is known by his speech and a wise man by silence.

Concern should drive us into action and not into a depression.

Learn silence. With the quiet serenity of a meditative mind, listen, absorb, transcribe, and transform.

The most momentous thing in human life is the art of winning the soul to good.

Allow not sleep to close your eyes three times reflecting on your actions of the day. What deeds done well, what not, what left undone?

Virtue is harmony.

Above all things, reverence yourself.

The art of living happily is to live in the present.

Strength of mind rests in sobriety, for this keeps your reason unclouded by passion.

The experience of life in a finite, limited body is specifically for the purpose of discovering and manifesting supernatural existence.

As long as man continues to be the ruthless destroyer of lower living beings, he will never know health or peace.

Numbers are the highest degree of knowledge. It is knowledge itself.

Choose always the way that seems the best, however rough it may be; custom will soon render it easy and agreeable.

Educate the children, and it won't be necessary to punish the men.

True and perfect friendship is to make one heart and mind of many hearts and bodies.

Man know thyself; then thou shalt known universe and God.

There is nothing so easy, but that it becomes difficult when you do it reluctantly.

Choose, rather be strong of soul than strong of body.

If you have a wounded heart, touch it as little as you would an injured eye. There are only two remedies for the suffering of the soul: hope and patience.

Above all things, respect yourself.

A thought is an idea in transit.

Choices are the hinges of destiny.

No man is free who cannot control himself.

Numbers rule the universe.

Astonishing! Everything is intelligent.

God built the universe on numbers.

Love that shines from within cannot be darkened by obstacles of the world of consequences.

There is no word or action but has its echo in eternity.

Richard Branson

The brave may not live forever, but the cautious do not live at all.

A business is simply an idea to make other people's lives better.

If your dreams don't scare you, they are too small.

There is no greater thing you can do with your life and your work than follow your passions in a way that serves the world and you.

The best way of learning about anything is by doing.

Entrepreneurship isn't just a label—it's a lifestyle.

The one person who can make your business succeed is not an investor or even a mentor; it is you.

An entrepreneur is an innovator, a job creator, a game-changer, a business leader, a disruptor, an adventurer.

The lesson that I have learned and follow all my life is that we should try and try and try again—but never give up!

Take a chance. It's the best way to test yourself. Have fun and push your boundaries.

My family brought me up to always look for the best in other people. I love people. I love spending time with people. I love learning from people.

Do not be embarrassed by your failures, learn from them, and start again.

You don't learn to walk by following rules. You learn by doing and falling over.

If you don't succeed at first, there's no need for the F word (Failure).
Pick yourself up and try, try again.

Entrepreneurship is a great leveler. The wonderful thing is that
money is not the sole currency when it comes to starting a business;
drive, determination, passion and hard work are all free and more
valuable than a pot of cash.

Don't be embarrassed by failures, learn from them, and start again.

Do good, have fun and the money will come.

Respect is how to treat everyone, not just those you want to impress.

Learn from failure. If you are an entrepreneur and your first venture
wasn't a success, welcome to the club.

My definition of success? The more you're actively and practically engaged, the more successful you will feel.

Happiness is the secret ingredient for successful businesses. If you have a happy company, it will be invincible.

Cover the downside.

When you're first thinking through an idea, it's important not to get bogged down in complexity. Thinking simply and clearly is hard to do.

Communication: the thing humans forgot when we invented words.

Your company should act as a springboard for ambitious employees, not a set of shackles.

If you don't have time for the small things, you won't have time for the big things.

Entrepreneurial business favors an open mind. It favors people whose optimism drives them to prepare for many possible futures, pretty much purely for the joy of doing so.

Listen. Take the best. Leave the rest.

If you spot an opportunity and are really excited by it, throw yourself into it with everything you've got.

Engage your emotions at work. Your instincts and emotions are there to help you.

Don't become a slave to technology, manage your phone, don't let it manage you.

A business has to be involving, it has to be fun, and it has to exercise your creative instincts.

You've got to take risks if you're going to succeed.

Train people well enough so they can leave; treat them well enough so they don't want to.

Please be polite. Nothing in life should erode the habit of saying, "Thank you," to people or praising them.

Entrepreneurship is about turning what excites you in life into capital so that you can do more of it and move forward with it.

Find the right people to work with, and you can't go wrong.

Remember, it's OK to be yourself.

Robert Kiyosaki

If you've failed, that means you're doing something. If you're doing something, you have a chance.

The size of your success is measured by the strength of your desire, the size of your dream, and how you handle disappointment along the way.

Successful people don't fear failure, but understand that it's necessary to learn and grow from.

Losers are people who are afraid of losing.

It's more important to grow your income than cut your expenses. It is more important to grow your spirit than cut your dreams.

Afraid of change? Then fail.

Money is not the goal. Money has no value. The value comes from the dreams money helps achieve.

When you are young, work to learn, not to earn.

The most successful people in life are the ones who ask questions. They're always learning. They're always growing. They're always pushing.

Remember, your mind is your greatest asset, so be careful what you put into it.

Broke is temporary; poor is eternal.

The richest people in the world build networks. Everyone else is trained to look for work.

Your mentors in life are important, so choose them wisely.

If you want to be rich think big, think differently.

Most people never get wealthy simply because they are not trained to recognize opportunities right in front of them.

The primary difference between rich people and poor people is how they handle fear.

Knowing you need to make a change isn't enough. You've got to find the guts to do it.

The money will never make you happy if you are an unhappy person.

Failure defeats losers; failure inspires winners.

I'd rather welcome change than cling to the past.

Don't let the fear of losing be greater than the excitement of winning.

Losers quit when they fail; winners fail until they succeed.

Successful people take big risks knowing that they might fall hard, but they might succeed more than they ever dreamed too.

Every time you think you can't do something, someone else thinks they can.

The difference between the rich and the poor is how they use their time.

How can I afford this? Change your words; change your life.

I keep hearing, 'I'd rather be happy than be rich.' Why not be both?

When you know you're right, you're not afraid of fighting back.

Don't waste a good mistake; learn from it.

Inside of every problem lies an opportunity.

Money only magnifies who you really are.

When you create wealth, it's your responsibility to return it to society.

One of the primary reasons why people struggle financially is because they cannot control their emotions of fear.

The thing I always say to people is this: If you avoid failure, you also avoid success.

Winners are not afraid of losing. Failure is part of the process of success.

Your future is created by what you do today, not tomorrow.

One of the reasons many people are not rich is because they are greedy.

Every successful person in life began by pursuing a passion, usually against all the odds.

Passion is the beginning of success.

The problem with this world is not enough problem solvers. So, if you become a problem solver, you become rich.

The poor, the unsuccessful, the unhappy, the unhealthy are the ones who use the word tomorrow the most.

Fail harder. You cannot be successful without failure.

The world is full of smart poor people.

Today is the word for winners, and tomorrow is the word for losers.

Complaining about your current position in life is worthless. Have a spine and do something about it instead.

The key to life is to be happy with or without money.

The philosophy of the rich and poor is this: the rich invest their money and spend what is left. The poor spend their money and invest what is left.

Dreamers dream dreams and rich people create plans and build bridges to their dreams.

Rich people buy luxuries last, while the poor and middle class tend to buy luxuries first.

Face your fears and doubts, and new worlds will open to you.

Confidence comes from discipline and training.

The sidelines are crowded. Get in the game.

Find out where you're at, where you're going and make a plan to get there.

If you're going to be a winner in life, you have to constantly go beyond your best.

Do today what you want for your tomorrows.

Don't work for money; make it work for you.

If you want to be rich, be friends with people who have the same mindset as you, or who at least won't try to change your mindset to be more like theirs. Life is too short to spend time with people who don't help you move forward.

A mistake is a signal that it is time to learn something new, something you didn't know before.

Sally Kristen Ride

All adventures, especially into new territory, are scary

After the Challenger accident, NASA put in a lot of time to improve the safety of the space shuttle to fix the things that had gone wrong.

But when I wasn't working, I was usually at a window looking down at Earth.

I felt very honored, and I knew that people would be watching very closely, and I felt it was very, very important that I do a good job.

I was always very interested in science, and I knew that for me, science was a better long-term career than tennis.

It takes a few years to prepare for a space mission.

It's easy to sleep floating around, it's very comfortable; but you have to be careful that you don't float into somebody or something!

Seneca

True happiness is to understand our duties toward God and man, to enjoy the present without anxious dependence upon the future, not to amuse ourselves with either hopes or fears, but to rest satisfied with what we have, which is abundantly sufficient.

As long as you live, keep learning how to live.

The bravest sight in the world is to see a great man struggling against adversity.

If one does not know to which port one is sailing, no wind is favorable.

Begin at once to live, and count each separate day as a separate life.

One of the most beautiful qualities of true friendship is to understand and to be understood.

Wealth is the slave of the wise, the master of the fool.

It is not the man who has too little, but the man who craves more, who is poor.

He who is brave is free.

He is most powerful who has power over himself.

Anger is like those ruins which smash themselves on what they fall.

Luck is a matter of preparation meeting opportunity.

No man was ever wise by chance.

It is the power of the mind to be unconquerable.

Time heals what reason cannot.

You want to live, but do you know how to live? You are scared of dying and tell me, is the kind of life you lead really any different from being dead?

Things that were hard to bear are sweet to remember.

Every night before going to sleep we must ask ourselves: what weakness did I overcome today? What virtue did I acquire?

If you wish to be loved, love.

Man is affected not by events, but by the view he takes of them.

A gem cannot be polished without friction, nor a man perfected without trials.

Throw me to the wolves, and I will return leading the pack.

Wherever there is a human being, there is an opportunity for kindness.

The only thing that belongs to us is time.

It is not because things are difficult that we do not dare; it is because we do not dare that things are difficult.

I am not born for one corner; the whole world is my native land.

We are more often frightened than hurt. We suffer more from imagination than from reality.

Time discovers the truth.

Sometimes even to live is an act of courage.

While we teach, we learn.

Everything that exceeds the bounds of moderation has an unstable

foundation.

Ignorance is the cause of fear.

It's not that we have a short time to live, but that we waste a lot of it.

Difficulties strengthen the mind, as labor does the body.

A man's as miserable as he thinks he is.

The greatest wealth is the poverty of desires.

While we are postponing, life speeds by.

Life is long if you know how to use it.

It is a rough road that leads to the heights of greatness.

Socrates

The only true wisdom is to know that you know nothing.

The secret of change is to focus all of your energy, not on fighting the old but on building the new.

True wisdom comes to each of us when we realize how little we understand about life, ourselves, and the world around us.

I call myself a peaceful warrior because the battles we fight are on the inside.

Those who are hardest to love need it the most.

Education is the kindling of a flame, not the filling of a vessel.

I cannot teach anybody anything; I can only make them think.

What screws us up the most in life is the picture in our heads of what it's supposed to be.

To move the world, we must first move.

Strong minds discuss ideas, average minds discuss events, weak minds discuss people.

Smart people learn from everything and everyone. Average people from their experiences. Stupid people already have all the answers.

Beware the barrenness of a busy life.

Wonder is the beginning of wisdom.

The secret of happiness is not found in seeking more, but in developing the capacity to enjoy less.

To find yourself, think for yourself.

Sometimes you put walls up not to keep people out, but to see who cares enough to break them down.

I know that I am intelligent because I know that I know nothing.

By all means, marry. If you get a good wife, you'll become happy. If you get a bad one, you'll become a philosopher.

There is no possession more valuable than a good and faithful friend.

I know you won't believe me, but the highest form of human excellence is to question oneself and others.

It's not living that matters, but living rightly.

Life is full of questions. Idiots are full of answers.

Understanding a question is half an answer.

One who is injured ought not to return the injury, for on no account can it be right to do an injustice; and it is not right to return an injury, or to do evil to any man, however much we have suffered from him.

Everyone wants to tell you what to do and what's good for you. They don't want you to find your own answers; they want you to believe theirs.

Be as you wish to seem.

From the deepest desires often come the deadliest hate.

An honest man is always a child.

He is rich, who is content with the least, for contentment is the wealth of nature.

Our prayers should be for blessings in general, for God knows best what is good for us.

He who is not contented with what he has would not be contented with what he would like to have.

Employ your time in improving yourself by other men's writings so that you shall gain easily what others have labored hard for.

Every action has its pleasure and its price.

Be nicer than necessary to everyone you meet. Everyone is fighting some kind of battle.

No man has the right to be an amateur in the matter of physical training. It is a shame for a man to grow old without seeing the beauty and strength of which his body is capable.

Remember, no human condition is ever permanent.

The value of a man is measured in the number of those who stand beside him, not those who follow.

True perfection is a bold quest to seek. Only the willing and true of heart will seek the betterment of many.

The mind is everything; what you think you become.

Sophia Loren

You have to enjoy life. Always be surrounded by people that you like, people who have a nice conversation. There are so many positive things to think about.

Nothing makes a woman more beautiful than the belief that she is beautiful.

Beauty is how you feel inside, and it reflects in your eyes. It is not something physical.

Mistakes are a part of the dues one pays for a full life.

When you are a mother, you are never really alone in your thoughts. A mother always has to think twice, once for herself and once for her child.

After all these years, I am still involved in the process of self-discovery. It's better to explore life and make mistakes than to play it safe. Mistakes are part of the dues one pays for a full life.

I have never judged myself by other people's standards. I have always expected a great deal of myself, and if I fail, I fail myself.

Everything you see I owe to spaghetti.

The facts of life are that a child who has seen war cannot be compared with a child who doesn't know what war is except television.

Any woman can look her best if she feels good in her skin. It's not a question of clothes or makeup. It's how she sparkles.

Sophie Kinsella

There's no luck in business. There's only drive, determination, and more drive.

If I've learned one lesson from all that's happened to me, it's that there is no such thing as the biggest mistake of your existence. There's no such thing as ruining your life. Life's a pretty resilient thing it turns out.

Look into your heart—and go after what you really want.

The thing with giving up is you never know. You never know whether you could have done the job. And I'm sick of not knowing about my life.

It's just the way things are, and you can't dwell on what might have been. You have to look at what is.

We all fail to appreciate each day just how much we already possess. Light, air, freedom, the companionship of friends.

The truth is, some relationships are supposed to last forever, and some are only supposed to last a few days. That's the way life is.

In the end, you have to choose whether or not to trust someone.

My life has changed, and I'm changing with it.

A real relationship is two way.

This is what happens. You tell your friends your most personal secrets, and they use them against you.

Never give up on anything you want. However impossible things may seem, there is always a way.

That's the way it goes. Some things happen, and some things don't. This one obviously just wasn't meant to be. Except, deep down, I still believe it was.

Steve Jobs

Stay hungry, stay foolish.

My job is not to be easy on people. My job is to make them better.

Don't let the noise of others' opinions drown out your own inner

voice.

I never did it for the money.

The journey is the reward.

If you are working on something exciting that you really care about,

you don't have to be pushed, the vision pulls you.

It's only by saying, "No," that you can concentrate on the things that are really important.

There is no reason not to follow your heart.

Innovation distinguishes between a leader and a follower

The only way to do great work is to love what you do

Be a yardstick of quality. Some people are not used to an environment where excellence is expected.

That's been one of my mantras—focus and simplicity. Simple can be harder than complex.

Great things in business are never done by one person. They're done by a team of people.

We don't get a chance to do that many things, and everyone should be really excellent. Because this is our life. Life is brief, and then you die, you know? So, this is what we've chosen to do with our life.

Think different.

Sometimes life will hit you in the head with a brick, don't lose faith.

If you haven't found what you want to do yet, keep looking. Don't settle.

We're here to put a dent in the universe.

It doesn't make sense to hire smart people and then tell them what to do; we hire smart people so they can tell us what to do.

My favorite things in life don't cost any money. It's really clear that the most precious resource we all have is time.

All I ask is that, today, you do the best work of your entire life.

Everyone here has the seen that right now is one of those moments when we are influencing the future.

Management is about persuading people to do things they do not want to, while leadership is about inspiring people to do things, they never thought they could.

If today was the last day of my life, would I want to do what I'm about to do today?

Don't let the noise of others' opinions drown out your own inner voice.

Design is not just how it looks and feels like. Design is how it works.

Let's go invent tomorrow rather than worrying about what happened yesterday.

People who know what they're talking about don't need PowerPoint.

Great things in business are never done by one person; they're done by a team of people.

Have the courage to follow your heart and intuition. They somehow know what you truly want to become.

You need to find what you love. And that is true both for your work and relationships.

Those who are crazy enough to think they can change the world usually do.

A brand is simply trusted.

I'm convinced that half of what separates the successful entrepreneurs from the non-successful ones is pure perseverance.

Your time is limited, so don't waste it living someone else's life.

Sun Tzu

Appear weak when you are strong and strong when you are weak.

Can you imagine what I would do if I could do all I can?

If you know the enemy and know yourself, you need not fear the results of a hundred battles.

Keep your friends close, your enemies even closer.

Know thy self, know thy enemy. A thousand battles, a thousand victories.

Every battle is won before it is fought

The supreme art of war is to subdue the enemy without fighting.

Let your plans be dark and as impenetrable as night, and when you move, fall like a thunderbolt.

If you are far from the enemy, make him believe you are near.

Victorious warriors win first and then go to war, while defeated warriors go to war first and then seek to win.

In the midst of chaos there is also opportunity.

The general who wins the battle makes many calculations in his temple before the battle is fought. The general who loses makes but few calculations beforehand.

Strategy without tactics is the slowest route to victory. Tactics without strategy are the noise before defeat.

Victory comes from finding opportunities in problems.

Do not engage an enemy more powerful than you,a nd if it is unavoidable and you do have to engage, then make sure you engage it on your terms, not on your enemy's terms.

If the mind is willing, the flesh could go on and on without many things.

Even the finest sword plunged into salt water will eventually rust.

Unhappy is the fate of one who tries to win his battles and succeed in his attacks without cultivating the spirit of enterprise, for the result is a waste of time and general stagnation.

A wise general makes a point of foraging of the enemy.

The good fighters of old first put themselves beyond the possibility of defeat and then waited for an opportunity of defeating the enemy.

All war is deception.

The greatest victory is that which requires no battle.

There is no instance of a nation benefiting from prolonged warfare.

Opportunities multiply as they are seized.

The quality of decision is like the well-timed swoop of a falcon, which enables it to strike and destroy its victim.

Thomas Edison

Never get discouraged if you fail. Learn from it. Keep trying.

Learn with both your head and hands.

Not everything of value in life comes from books—experience the world.

Never stop learning. Read the entire panorama of literature.

Our greatest weakness lies in giving up. The most certain way to succeed is always to try just one more time.

Just because something doesn't do what you planned it to do doesn't mean it's useless.

There is no substitute for hard work.

I have not failed. I've just found 10,000 ways that won't work.

If we did all the things, we are capable of, we would literally astound ourselves.

What you are will show in what you do.

Opportunity is missed by most people because it is dressed in overalls and looks like work.

The three great essentials to achieve anything worthwhile are hard work, stick-to-itiveness, and common sense.

Maturity is often more absurd than youth and very frequently is most unjust to youth.

Genius is one percent inspiration and ninety-nine percent perspiration.

I never did a day's work in my life. It was all fun.

Being busy does not always mean real work. The object of all work is production or accomplishment, and to either of these ends, there must be forethought, system, planning, intelligence, and honest purpose, as well as perspiration. Seeming to do is not doing.

I have friends in overalls whose friendship I would not swap for the favor of the kings of the world.

Everything comes to him who hustles while he waits.

I never did anything by accident, nor did any of my inventions come by accident; they came by work.

Nearly every man who develops an idea works it up to the point where it looks impossible, and then he gets discouraged. That's not the place to become discouraged.

To invent, you need a good imagination and a pile of junk.

Hell, there are no rules here—we're trying to accomplish something.

Waste is worse than loss. The time is coming when every person who lays claim to ability will keep the question of waste before him constantly. The scope of thrift is limitless.

Restlessness is discontent, and discontent is the first necessity of progress. Show me a thoroughly satisfied man and I will show you a failure.

Be courageous. I have seen many depressions in business. Always America has emerged from these stronger and more prosperous. Be as brave as your fathers before you. Have faith! Go forward!

The chief function of the body is to carry the brain around.

Many of life's failures are people who did not realize how close they were to success when they gave up.

There's a way to do it better—find it.

Your worth consists in what you are and not in what you have.

There will one day spring from the brain of science a machine or force so fearful in its potentialities, so absolutely terrifying, that even man, the fighter, who will dare torture and death in order to inflict torture and death, will be appalled, and so abandon war forever.

The best thinking has been done in solitude. The worst has been done in turmoil.

To have a great idea, have a lot of them.

The value of an idea lies in the using of it.

Show me a thoroughly satisfied man, and I will show you a failure.

Thomas More

You wouldn't abandon ship in a storm just because you couldn't control the winds.

An absolutely new idea is one of the rarest things known to man.

A pretty face may be enough to catch a man, but it takes a character and good nature to hold him.

One of the greatest problems of our time is that many are schooled, but few are educated.

If honor were profitable, everybody would be honorable.

It is naturally given to all men to esteem their own inventions best.

I would uphold the law if for no other reason but to protect myself.

They have no lawyers among them, for they consider them as a sort of people whose profession it is to disguise matters.

Our emotional symptoms are precious sources of life and individuality.

What is deferred is not avoided.

For if you suffer your people to be ill-educated, and their manners to be corrupted from their infancy, and then punish them for those crimes to which their first education disposed of them, what else is to be concluded from this but that you first make thieves and then punish them?

It is a wise man's part, rather avoid sickness, than to wish for medicines.

Instead of inflicting these horrible punishments, it would be far more to the point to provide everyone with some means of livelihood, so that nobody's under the frightful necessity of becoming first a thief and then a corpse.

Nobody owns anything, but everyone is rich—for what greater wealth can there be than cheerfulness, peace of mind, and freedom from anxiety?

A man taking basil from a woman will love her always.

If we lived in a state where virtue was profitable, common sense would make us saintly. But since we see that avarice, anger, pride, and stupidity commonly profit far beyond charity, modesty, justice, and thought, perhaps we must stand fast a little, even at the risk of being heroes.

One man to live in pleasure and wealth, whiles all other weep and smart for it, that is the part not of a king, but of a jailor.

The Utopians feel that slaughtering our fellow creatures gradually destroys the sense of compassion, which is the finest sentiment of which our human nature is capable.

For when they see the people swarm into the streets, and daily wet to the skin with rain, and yet cannot persuade them to go out of the rain, they do keep themselves within their houses, seeing they cannot remedy the folly of the people.

They wonder much to hear that gold, which in itself is so useless a thing, should be everywhere so much esteemed; that even men for whom it was made, and by whom it has its value, should yet be thought of less value than it is.

What though youth gave love and roses, age still leaves us friends and wine

Warren Edward Buffett

Someone is sitting in the shade today because someone planted a tree a long time ago.

Risk comes from not knowing what you're doing.

Predicting rain doesn't count. Building arks does.

Wall Street is the only place that people ride to in a Rolls Royce to get advice from those who take the subway.

Should you find yourself in a chronically leaking boat, energy devoted to changing vessels is likely to be more productive than energy devoted to patching leaks.

The first rule is not to lose. The second rule is not to forget the first rule.

In the business world, the rearview mirror is always clearer than the windshield.

It's far better to buy a wonderful company at a fair price than a fair company at a wonderful price.

I think that both parties should declare the debt limit as a political weapon of mass destruction which can't be used. I mean, it is silly to have a country that has 237 years building up its reputation and then have people threaten to tear it down because they're not getting some other matter.

The rich are always going to say that, you know, just give us more money, and we'll go out and spend more and then it will all trickle down to the rest of you. But that has not worked the last 10 years, and I hope the American public is catching on.

Only when the tide goes out do you discover who's been swimming naked.

The only way to get love is to be lovable. It's very irritating if you have a lot of money. You'd like to think you could write a check, "I'll buy a million dollars' worth of love." But it doesn't work that way. The more you give love away, the more you get.

Will Smith

The first step is you have to say you can.

Throughout life, people will make you mad, disrespect you and treat you bad. Let God deal with the things they do, 'cause hate in your heart will consume you too.

I've always considered myself to be just average talent, and what I have is a ridiculous insane obsessiveness for practice and preparation.

And where I excel is ridiculous, sickening, work ethic. You know, while the other guy's sleeping? I'm working.

Money and success don't change people; they merely amplify what is already there.

Whatever your dream is, every extra penny you have needs to be going to that.

I've trained myself to illuminate the things in my personality that are likable and to hide and protect the things that are less likable.

I'm a student of patterns. At heart, I'm a physicist. I look at everything in my life as trying to find the single equation, the theory of everything.

The things that have been most valuable to me I did not learn in school.

If you're not willing to work hard, let someone else do it. I'd rather be with someone who does a horrible job but gives 110% than with someone who does a good job and gives 60%.

When you create art, the world has to wait.

You can cry, ain't no shame in it.

I have a great time with my life, and I want to share it.

Life is lived on the edge.

I know how to learn anything I want to learn. I absolutely know that I could learn how to fly the space shuttle because someone else knows how to fly it, and they put it in a book. Give me the book, and I do not need somebody to stand up in front of the class.

For me, there is nothing more valuable than how people feel in a movie theater about a movie.

So, if you stay ready, you ain't got to get ready, and that is how I run my life.

I want the world to be better because I was here.

Traditional education is based on facts and figures and passing tests—not on a comprehension of the material and its application to your life.

Fear kills your ability to see beauty.

I'm a student of world religion, so to me, it's hugely important to have the knowledge and to understand what people are doing.

I think with movies; I am really connecting to Joseph Campbell's idea of the collective unconscious.

I don't know what my calling is, but I want to be here for a bigger reason. I strive to be like the greatest people who have ever lived.

William Shakespeare

We know what we are, but know not what we may be.

Give every man thy ear but few thy voice.

Love me or hate me, both are in my favor. If you love me, I'll always be in your heart; if you hate me, I'll always be in your mind.

I always feel happy, you know why? Because I don't expect anything from anyone, expectations always hurt. Life is short, so love your life, be happy and keep smiling.

Have more than you show, speak less than you know.

Just live for yourself, and before you speak, listen. Before you write, think. Before you spend, earn. Before you pray, forgive. Before you hurt, feel. Before you hate, love. Before you quit, try. Before you die, live.

To do a great right, do a little wrong.

There is nothing either good or bad, but thinking makes it so.

God has given you one face, and you make yourself another.

Love all, trust a few, do wrong to none.

Always the wrong person gives you the right lesson in life.

Knowledge is the wing wherewith we fly to heaven.

Words are easy, like the wind; faithful friends are hard to find.

Time is very slow for those who wait, very fast for those who are scared, very long for those who celebrate; but for those who love, time is eternal.

No legacy is so rich as honesty.

If money goes before, all ways do lie open.

A friend is one that knows you as you are, understands where you have been, accepts what you have become, and still gently allows you to grow.

All the worlds a stage, and all the men and women merely players. They have their exits and their entrances, and one man in his time plays many parts.

Some are born great, some achieve greatness, and some have greatness thrust upon them.

The eyes are the window to your soul.

If to do were as easy to know what we're well to do.

Love looks not with the eyes but with the mind.

Speak what we feel, not what we ought to say.

Life's but a walking shadow, a poor player that struts and frets his hour upon the stage, and then is heard no more; it is a tale told by an idiot, full of sound and fury, signifying nothing.

The expectation is the root of all heartache.

Things done well and with a care exempt themselves from fear.

There is no darkness but ignorance.

Talking isn't doing. It is a kind of good deed to say well, and yet words are not deeding.

Cowards die many times before their deaths; the valiant never taste of death but once.

Winston Churchill

To build may have to be the slow and laborious task of years. To destroy can be the thoughtless act of a single day.

The farther backward you can look, the farther forward you are likely to see.

There are a terrible lot of lies going about the world, and the worst of it is that half of them are true.

All the greatest things are simple, and many can be expressed in a single word: freedom, justice, honor, duty, mercy, hope.

One ought never to turn one's back on a threatened danger and try to run away from it. If you do that, you will double the danger. But, if you meet it promptly and without flinching, you will reduce the danger by half.

The price of greatness is responsibility.

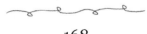

Broadly speaking, short words are best, and the old words, when short, are best of all.

Attitude is a little thing that makes a big difference.

To improve is to change, so to be perfect is to change often.

If you're going through hell, keep going.

Courage is what it takes to stand up and speak; it's also what it takes to sit down and listen.

We shall not fail or falter. We shall not weaken or tire. Neither the sudden shock of battle nor the long-drawn trials of vigilance and exertion will wear us down. Give us the tools, and we will finish the job.

Out of intense complexities, intense simplicities emerge.

Those who can win a war well can rarely make a good peace, and those who could make a good peace would never have won the war.

Never hold discussions with the monkey when the organ grinder is in the room.

The first duty of the university is to teach wisdom, not a trade; character, not technicalities. We want a lot of engineers in the modern world, but we do not want a world of engineers.

Courage is rightly esteemed the first of human qualities because, it has been said, it is the quality which guarantees all others.

This is the lesson: never give in, never give in, never, never, never, never—in nothing, great or small, large or petty—never give in except to convictions of honor and good sense. Never yield to force; never yield to the apparently overwhelming might of the enemy.

It's not enough that we do our best; sometimes we have to do what's required.

Yoko Ono

What the Beatles did was something incredible; it was more than what a band could do. We have to give them respect.

The regret of my life is that I have not said 'I love you' often enough.

Smile in the mirror. Do that every morning, and you'll start to see a big difference in your life.

The mirror becomes a razor when it's broken. A stick becomes a flute when it's loved.

What we do really affects the world. Most of us think we can't do anything, but it really isn't true.

The nice thing about the gallery shows is that without having to pay any money, you can just go and see it.

Art is a way of survival.

Life with another person is always difficult.

What is beauty? It's what you love.

Our thoughts determine our age.

Don't ever give up on life. Life can be so beautiful, especially after you've spent a lot of time with it.

When you are suffering, you become more understanding of yourself, but also about other people's sufferings too. That's the first step to understanding somebody is to understand their sufferings. So then love follows.

I'm not going to doubt my life.

If your life changes, we can change the world too.

Every drop in the ocean counts.

In your head, a sunset can go on for days

Try to say nothing negative about anybody. a) for three days b) for forty-five days c) for three months. See what happens to your life.

Spring passes and one remembers one's innocence. Summer passes and one remembers one's exuberance. Autumn passes and one remembers one's reverence. Winter passes and one remembers one's perseverance.

You may think I'm small, but I have a universe inside my mind.

We've been filled with great treasure for one purpose: to be spilled.

You change the world by being yourself.

A dream you dream alone may be a dream, but a dream two people dream together is a reality.

Grow love with me.

Some people are old at 18, and some are young at 90. Time is a concept that humans created.

Imagine a dolphin dancing in the sky. Let it dance with joy. Think of yourself at the bottom of the ocean watching.

All my life, I have been in love with the sky. Even when everything was falling apart around me, the sky was always there for me.

Every moment in our lives is a miracle we should enjoy instead of ignoring.

Tape the sound of the moon fading at dawn. Give it to your mother to listen to when she's in sorrow.

Made in United States
Orlando, FL
14 June 2022

18816291R00098